Across Cultures

中西文化面对面

地理篇 ★ PLACES

中英双语版

小学中高年级适用（配动画视频）

（澳）詹姆斯·宾
（澳）吉莉安·法拉蒂
樊　琳
张园勤

编著

上海教育出版社
SHANGHAI EDUCATIONAL
PUBLISHING HOUSE

图书在版编目（CIP）数据

中西文化面对面.地理篇：英汉对照/（澳）詹姆斯·宾，（澳）吉莉安·法拉蒂编著；张园勤译.—上海：上海教育出版社，2020.9
ISBN 978-7-5720-0202-1

Ⅰ.①中… Ⅱ.①詹… ②吉… ③张… Ⅲ.①英语课–小学–课外读物 Ⅳ.① G624.313

中国版本图书馆 CIP 数据核字 (2020) 第 127985 号

策划编辑：林　妍
责任编辑：戴嘉子
封面设计：朱博韡

中西文化面对面·地理篇
（澳）詹姆斯·宾　（澳）吉莉安·法拉蒂　编著
樊琳　张园勤

出版发行	上海教育出版社有限公司
网　　址	www.seph.com.cn
	www.centuryenglish.com
地　　址	上海永福路123号
邮　　编	200031
印　　刷	上海昌鑫龙印务有限公司
开　　本	787×1092　1/16　印张 5.75
版　　次	2020年9月第 1 版
印　　次	2020年9月第 1 次印刷
书　　号	ISBN 978-7-5720-0202-1/G·0158
定　　价	35.80元

如发现质量问题，读者可向本社调换　　电话：021-64377165

前　　言

　　亲爱的小读者们，你了解哪些著名的城市？你知道他们都承载着怎样的历史内涵和文化底蕴？你想不想足不出户就能领略中外名城胜地的魅力？本书将带给你全新的中西地理文化体验。

　　在这本书里，来自波波星的宇航员吉姆（Jim）、萨拉（Sara）和智能助手小白（Bio）将和你一起探索多彩城市和观光胜地，在不同主题场景下，通过对比的形式了解中西城市文化和名胜古迹。

　　来看看每个单元里都有些什么吧！

情景导入　　看漫画，了解这个单元是什么主题。扫描页面上的二维码还有动画视频可以看哦。

阅读篇章　　中英双语的阅读语篇，带你领略中外著名城市和名胜古迹的方方面面。

小小测试　　和文化相关的小练习，看看你都了解了吗？

主题词汇　　和文化相关的主题词汇，便于理解与记忆。

语汇积累　　常用的英语好词好句，助你成为英语小达人。

文化发现　　新奇有趣的内容开阔你的眼界，拓宽你的文化视野。

问题思考　　开动脑筋，找到你自己的答案吧。

　　本书内容丰富有趣，让你在了解中西方文化差异的同时，逐步形成文化包容的态度，增强跨文化意识，提升思辨能力，也能帮助你提高中英文阅读能力和跨文化交际能力哦！快和三位新伙伴一起来探索和发现中西地理文化的无穷魅力吧！

本书编写组

2020 年 7 月

Contents

Chapter 1

Wonderful Cities
多彩城市

扫码观看完整视频

Unit 1
Beijing
北京

We are going to China. Our first stop is Beijing, the capital of China.

Beijing

Beijing, China's capital, is an ancient city. It is rich in history and culture. For visitors, there is a lot to see.

Beijing's most famous landmark is the Palace Museum. It is in the center of the city. It is about 600 years old. It was the home of Chinese emperors during the Ming Dynasty and the Qing Dynasty—from the early 15th century to the early 20th century.

The Palace Museum is a UNESCO World Heritage Site. Thousands of tourists visit it each day. They come to see the historical buildings and beautiful works of art.

The Summer Palace is a famous park in Beijing. It is also called the Museum of Royal Gardens. Visitors can enjoy views of peaceful gardens, a large lake, and many old buildings. The Summer Palace is also a UNESCO World Heritage Site.

北 京

　　中国首都北京是一座古老的城市，有着悠久的历史与丰富的文化。对旅游者来说，有许多值得一去的地方。

　　北京最著名的标志性建筑是故宫博物院。它坐落在北京的中心。故宫博物院有约 600 年的历史，在 15 世纪初至 20 世纪初明清年间，它曾是历代皇帝的居所。

　　故宫博物院被联合国教科文组织列为世界遗产地。每天都有无数游客前来参观，游览富有历史意义的建筑，观赏精美的艺术品。

　　颐和园是北京的一座著名园林，也被称为"中国皇家园林博物馆"。在这里，游客可以徜徉在宁静的花园中，观赏无垠的湖水，游览许多古代建筑。颐和园也被联合国教科文组织列为世界遗产地。

Beijing Opera is a traditional art form. It is a combination of music, singing, dancing, acting, acrobatics and colorful costumes. In Beijing Opera, there are four types of characters. The Sheng characters are men. The Dan characters are women. The Jing and the Chou characters have painted faces. The Jing characters are strong men and the Chou characters are funny men.

In 2008, Beijing hosted the Summer Olympic Games. The city built two big new landmarks for the Games. The "Bird's Nest" is the National Stadium. It has the shape of a bird's nest. The "Water Cube" is the swimming center. Its walls look like water bubbles. In 2022, Beijing will host the Winter Olympic Games.

京剧是一种传统艺术，它融合了音乐、歌唱、舞蹈、表演、杂技以及色彩绚丽的服装道具。在京剧里，一共有四种角色："生角"是男性角色；"旦角"是女性角色；"净角"与"丑角"都画有脸谱，"净角"是勇猛的男性，"丑角"则是逗趣的男性。

2008 年，北京举办了夏季奥运会。为了迎接此次盛会，北京建造了两座地标性建筑。鸟巢是国家体育馆，它的形状就像一个鸟的窝巢。水立方是游泳中心，它的外墙看起来像是由许多水泡组成的。2022 年，北京还将举办冬季奥运会。

Quiz 小小测试

(   ) 1. This is the picture of a _____.

      A. Sheng character   B. Dan character

      C. Jing character   D. Chou character

(   ) 2. What can people see in the Palace Museum?

      A. Historical buildings.   B. Works of art.   C. A large lake.

(   ) 3. What can people see in the Summer Palace?

      A. A large lake.   B. A big square.   C. Peaceful gardens.

4. Match the pictures with the correct description.

●   ● the swimming centre

●   ● the National Stadium

Topic Vocabulary 主题词汇

the Palace Museum 故宫博物院

the Qing Dynasty 清朝

World Heritage Site 世界遗产地

the Museum of Royal Gardens 皇家花园博物馆

the Summer Olympic Games 夏季奥运会

the National Stadium 国家体育馆

the Water Cube 水立方

the Winter Olympic Games 冬季奥运会

the Ming Dynasty 明朝

UNESCO 联合国教科文组织

The Summer Palace 颐和园

Beijing Opera 京剧

the Bird's Nest 鸟巢

Useful Expressions 语汇积累

in the centre of ... 在……的中心

the early 15th century 15 世纪初

works of art 艺术品

a combination of ... ……的融合

It is rich in history and culture. 它有着悠久的历史与丰富的文化。

Visitors can enjoy views of peaceful gardens, a large lake, and many old buildings. 游客可以徜徉在宁静的花园中，观赏无垠的湖水，游览许多古代建筑。

It has the shape of a bird's nest. 它的形状就像一个鸟的窝巢。

Culture Discovery 文化发现

北京四合院

北京是中国的首都，拥有的名胜古迹数量巨大，如故宫、十三陵、颐和园等，其他城市"望城莫及"。

北京也是中国的政治文化中心。由于不同民族长期在北京聚集、生活、交流，最终形成了独有的雅俗共赏的多元文化，对全国各地的老百姓都极具吸引力。

今时今日的北京高楼林立。但说起北京，就必须提一下明清时代扎根发展的"四合院"。虽说四合院是以前北京人居住的普通房子，但蕴含着丰富的文化内涵。四合院属于比较规整的建筑类型，闻名遐迩，故宫以及老北京胡同里的住宅都是四合院的代表。四合院这个名字就代表了它的设计内涵，"四"指四面建有房屋，"合"指将院子围合在中间。

为什么老百姓喜欢住在四合院里呢？因为其优势显而易见。四面的房屋都相对独立，即便是一大家子住里面，也可以拥有一定的空间和隐私，但彼此之间又紧密地连接在了一起，

颐和园

四合院

10

能够互帮互助，起居十分便利。中心的庭院兼具采光、通风、休息、交流、家务劳动等功能，平日大家在院子里闲聊几句，唠唠家常，互道晚安，增进了彼此的感情。

在北京，你既可以漫步在西单、王府井等商业中心，逛累了坐在现代化的写字楼里喝杯咖啡，也可以去十三陵、八达岭等转转，或者提着鸟笼在天桥转悠。如果你选择后者，说不定还能让你有种穿越的感觉，这种厚重的年代感恐怕是北京和其他历史古都才特有的吧。

Think and Answer 问题思考

1. 说到北京胡同里的四合院就会让人联想到上海弄堂里的石库门，你知道它们有些什么异同吗？
2. 你听说过"老北京文化"吗？能简单描述一下吗？

十三陵

王府井大街

扫码观看完整视频

Unit 2
Shanghai
上海

Shanghai

Shanghai is one of the largest cities in the world. There are many interesting places to visit in Shanghai. The city is an interesting mix of old and new.

One of the most famous tourist destinations is the Bund. This waterfront area has many historical buildings in different architectural styles. Tourists and locals come here on summer evenings to walk beside the Huangpu River.

Yu Garden is a traditional Chinese garden. There are many beautiful buildings, bridges, and ponds in the garden. Visitors can enjoy its natural beauty. They can buy everything from traditional oil-paper umbrellas to delicious snacks such as *xiaolongbao* at the Yuyuan market nearby.

Traditional Shanghai is still alive. You can still find longtang. In the past, many families lived together in each longtang. They helped each other. They shared meals and talked together in the evenings. Children played games such as marbles and rolling hoops outside. Today, fewer people live in the longtang. They are much quieter than before.

上海

上海是世界上最大的城市之一。这里有许多值得参观的有趣景点。这是一座古老与现代交融的城市。

上海最著名的旅游景点之一是外滩。滨江拥有不同风格的历史建筑群。在夏夜，游客和当地人喜欢来到这里，沿着黄浦江散步。

豫园是一座传统的中式园林。这里有许多漂亮的建筑、小桥和池塘。游客能在此领略自然之美。在附近的豫园商城，无论是传统的油纸伞还是小笼包之类的美味小吃，游客几乎什么都能买得到。

老上海依然存在，例如弄堂。旧时，每一条弄堂里都住着多户人家。邻里之间会互相帮助。在晚上，他们一起吃饭、聊天。孩子们则在外面玩着打弹珠和滚铁环之类的游戏。如今，住在弄堂里的人越来越少。和以前相比，弄堂显得安静了许多。

Shanghai is also a modern city and cultural center. In 2010, it hosted the largest-ever World Expo. The theme of the Expo was "Better City, Better Life." One hundred and ninety-two countries took part. About 73 million people visited the Expo!

The city is also famous for the Shanghai International Film Festival. This festival started in 1993. Filmmakers from many countries come to the festival. People can enjoy the latest films from around the world.

Shanghai is an exciting city filled with history, beauty, and culture.

上海也是一座现代化的城市和文化中心。2010年，上海举办了盛况空前的世博会。此次世博会的主题是"城市，让生活更美好"。共有192个国家参加了上海世博会，参观者达7300万人次。

"上海国际电影节"也闻名遐迩。电影节始办于1993年，世界各国的电影人共赴盛会。在电影节上，人们能够观赏全球最新的电影。

上海是一座集历史底蕴、美丽风情与文化魅力于一体的精彩纷呈的城市。

 **小小测试**

(   ) 1. We can buy traditional oil-paper umbrellas at _____.

A. The Yuyuan market   B. the Bund

2. Look and match.

                          ●   ● The Bund

                          ●   ● Longtang

                          ●   ● Expo China Pavilion

                          ●   ● Shanghai International
                                                                            Film Festival

                          ●   ● Yu Garden

Topic Vocabulary 主题词汇

the Bund 外滩

Yu Garden 豫园

xiaolongbao 小笼包

marbles and rolling hoops 弹珠和滚铁圈

World Expo 世界博览会（简称"世博会"）

the Shanghai International Film Festival 上海国际电影节

the Huangpu River 黄浦江

oil-paper umbrella 油纸伞

longtang 弄堂

Useful Expressions 语汇积累

tourist destination 旅游景点

natural beauty 自然之美

delicious snacks 美味小吃

take part 参加

from around the world 来自世界各地

The city is an interesting mix of old and new. 这是一座古老与现代交融的城市。

This waterfront area has many historical buildings in different architectural styles. 滨江区域有着不同风格的历史建筑群。

Shanghai is an exciting city filled with history, beauty, and culture. 上海是一座集历史底蕴、美丽风情与文化魅力于一体的精彩纷呈的城市。

Culture Discovery 文化发现

上海风情

　　上海位于中国海岸线中部长江口，地理位置得天独厚。来自中国各地，甚至世界各地的人们汇聚在此地学习、工作、生活，同时也带来了自己家乡的文化和习俗，而这也涵养了上海海纳百川、兼容并蓄的城市精神。但与此同时，也保留了很多具有浓厚老上海风情的传统，比如弄堂文化、沪剧、滑稽戏等。

　　要深刻体会上海风情，一定要去那些闻名遐迩的文艺浪漫街走走。首推武康路，北起华山路，南至淮海中路，全长不过一公里多一点，但无数社会名流和普通老百姓都钟情于武康路。一方面源于小街上多处具有异国风情的历史建筑；另一方面是因为小街独特的气质，静谧、端庄、悠闲、风情万种，难怪著名导演李安也对武康路情有独钟。阳光明媚时，在武康路散个步，喝杯咖啡，逛一下各种特色小店，都能令人身心满足。除了武康路，还有很多充满文艺气息的小街或弄堂，如多伦路文化名人街、陕西路历史文化街、田子坊等都在等着你去探索。

武康路

弄堂

　　因为上海是中国现代化的代表城市之一，所以人们很容易忘了上海其实还有老街文化。如果你有兴趣去上海老街走走，那选择也是相当丰富的，比如七宝老街，广场石碑坊上的"北宋遗存"诉说着老街悠久的历史。青浦的朱家角有着上海保存较好的明清建筑一条街及典型的江南水乡风景，两岸古老的民宅和各色小店呈现了旺盛的生命力。还有浦东的川沙老街，也是保存较好的百年老街。去川沙老街不能错过那里的古城墙公园，里面有一段近80米长的嘉靖年间的古城墙遗迹，距今已有400多年的历史。老街保留了上海早年市井生活的质朴原型和深受本地人欢迎的小食。比起朱家角和七宝，这里的人流量并不大，能让人放慢脚步，体会小街的古朴风格。

Think and Answer 问题思考

1. 你对"海派文化"了解多少？你觉得海派文化是上海独有的吗？
2. 考考你，上海有多少世界非物质文化遗产？请举例说明。

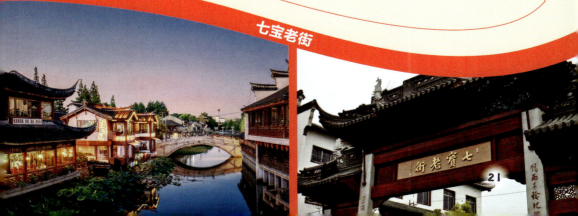

七宝老街

21

Unit 3
New York
纽约

New York

New York is called "the city that never sleeps". Over 8 million people live there. More than 54 million people visit it each year. There are many exciting places to visit in New York.

Times Square is famous for its huge electronic billboards. In Times Square the lights never go out. It is always crowded—day and night. People go there to eat, shop, walk, and enjoy the excitement. On New Year's Eve over a million people gather together in Times Square. They go there for the famous countdown to the New Year. At midnight there are balloons, music, and fireworks.

纽 约

纽约被称为"不夜城"，拥有超过 800 万人口。每年前来参观的人数更是超过 5400 万。纽约有许多值得一去的地方。

时代广场因为其巨大的电子广告牌而闻名遐迩。在时代广场，灯光长明不熄。广场上不分昼夜人潮涌动。人们到那吃饭、购物、散步，尽享欢乐时光。在新年前夜，超过 100 万人聚集在时代广场，参加著名的新年倒计时活动。午夜时分，气球放飞，音乐奏响，烟花燃放。

This is the famous Broadway. More than 12 million people go to a show there each year. The first theatre in New York opened in 1750. Today there are 40 theatres on Broadway. Some of the most famous Broadway musicals are *Cats*, *Mamma Mia*, and *The Lion King*. *The Phantom of the Opera* is the longest-running musical in the world. It opened on Broadway in 1988 and is still on today.

The Statue of Liberty stands on Liberty Island in New York Harbor. The people of France gave the statue to the people of the United States in 1886. The statue is holding a torch and a tablet. On the tablet there is an important date: July 4, 1776. This is the date of *the American Declaration of Independence*. About 4 million people visit the statue each year.

这就是著名的百老汇。每年都会有超过 1200 万的观众去那里观看演出。纽约的第一家剧院于 1750 年开张,如今在百老汇已经有 40 家剧院了。百老汇最著名的音乐剧包括《猫》《妈妈咪呀》和《狮子王》。《歌剧魅影》是世界上连续上演时间最长的音乐剧。它于 1988 年在百老汇首演,直至目前依然活跃在舞台上。

自由女神像矗立在纽约港的自由岛上。1886 年,法国人民将这座雕像赠送给美国。女神像一手举着火炬,一手拿着石碑。石碑上记载了一个重要的日子:1776 年 7 月 4 日。这是美国《独立宣言》的发表日。每年有大约 400 万游客前来参观这座雕像。

Quiz 小小测试

1. Look and match.

  • Cats

 • Mamma Mia

 • The Lion King

 • The Phantom of the Opera

(　　) 2. On New Year's Eve over a million people gather together in _____.

A. Times Square　　　　B. Broadway

(　　) 3. You can go to a performance of opera at _____.

A. The Statue of Liberty　　　　B. Broadway

(　　) 4. What does the Statue of Liberty hold?

　　A　　　　B　　　　C　　　　D

Topic Vocabulary 主题词汇

Times Square 时代广场

countdown to the New Year 新年倒数

Cats《猫》

The Lion King《狮子王》

the Statue of Liberty 自由女神像

New York Harbor 纽约港

the American Declaration of Independence《独立宣言》

huge electronic billboards 大型电子公告牌

Broadway 百老汇（美国纽约街道名）

Mamma Mia《妈妈咪呀》

The Phantom of the Opera《歌剧魅影》

Liberty Island 自由岛

Useful Expressions 语汇积累

the city that never sleeps 不夜城

be famous for ... 以……闻名

day and night 不分昼夜

enjoy the excitement 尽享欢乐时光

gather together 聚集在一起

In Times Square the lights never go out. 在时代广场，灯光长明不熄。

The Phantom of the Opera is the longest-running musical in the world.《歌剧魅影》是世界上连续上演时间最长的音乐剧。

Culture Discovery 文化发现

纽约魅力

纽约，无疑是美国最光鲜亮丽的城市之一。那么纽约独特的魅力来源于什么呢？除了前文中提到的时代广场、百老汇和自由女神像以外，还必须提一下著名的华尔街和中央公园，它们体现了纽约的城市竞争力和艺术气质。

华尔街是曼哈顿区南部的一条大街，以美国金融中心著称。华尔街可谓是美国经济的"心脏"，也是金融从业人员心中的神殿。华尔街的标志是一头重达3吨多的铜牛雕塑，它是"力量和勇气"的象征。每天都有无数来自世界各地的游客慕名前来排队和这头"名牛"合影，希望给自己带来冲天"牛"运。

同样位于市区的中央公园被称为纽约的后花园，它面积340公顷，占150个街区。150个街区有多大呢？中央公园沿街而建，如果你沿着公园的一边走，需要走过整整150条横马路才会到公园的尽头。中央公园内有不少著名的景点，比如：戴拉寇特剧院（Delacorte Theater），每逢夏季都会举办莎士比亚戏剧节，人们会聚在露天的剧场一睹《驯悍记》《无事

纽约中央公园

华尔街

生非》等莎翁名剧；还有被誉为"童话城堡"的瞭望台古堡（Belvedere Castle），设计并建于 1800 年，belvedere 是意大利语，意思是"美丽的景色"，古堡里面有一个天文台，为青少年们提供望远镜等器材，供他们探索自然。

中央公园附近博物馆汇集，有大都会艺术博物馆、惠特妮美术馆、古根海姆美术馆等等，是艺术爱好者的天堂。另外，还有美国自然历史博物馆。从外表看，它是一座综合罗马与文艺复兴样式的雄伟建筑，因为是《博物馆奇妙夜》《侏罗纪公园》等大片的拍摄地，每年吸引着无数自然和电影爱好者前往朝圣。

纽约海纳百川，是多元文化大熔炉的典范。纽约作为移民城市，各种肤色、民族、信仰的人聚集在一起，有融合、有碰撞，追逐梦想。

Think and Answer 问题思考

1. 你知道纽约还有哪些地标？你最喜爱其中哪一个？为什么？
2. 纽约的生活节奏快，竞争激烈，你愿意在这样的城市工作和生活吗？为什么？

大都会艺术博物馆

Unit 4
London
伦敦

London

London is the capital of the United Kingdom. Millions of tourists go there every year. There is a lot to see and do in this interesting old city. It has museums, parks, and old buildings.

The river is the Thames. It runs through the center of London. There are many bridges across the Thames. The most famous is this one, Tower Bridge. It is over 120 years old. The bridge goes between two towers. When ships need to pass, it opens up.

That old castle beside the river and next to Tower Bridge is called the Tower of London. It was a prison for over 800 years. Some of England's kings and queens spent time in prison there.

伦 敦

　　伦敦是英国的首都。每年有数百万的游客前往那里旅游。在这个古老而有趣的城市里，有很多值得一看的地方，也有很多值得一试的事情。伦敦有许多博物馆、公园与古建筑。

　　这就是泰晤士河，它贯穿伦敦市中心。河上横亘着多座桥梁。其中最著名的当属塔桥，它已经有超过120年的历史了。桥的主体坐落在两座塔楼中间。当轮船要经过时，桥面就会打开。

　　泰晤士河旁边，紧临着塔桥的那座古老的城堡叫作伦敦塔。它曾是一座监狱，有超过800年的历史。一些英国的国王和王后曾经被拘禁在那里。

That's the Palace of Westminster. It is another famous building beside the Thames. This grand building has a tall tower with a clock at the top. It is called Big Ben. Every hour, Big Ben rings to tell the time. Four smaller bells ring every fifteen minutes.

Buckingham Palace is the home of the Queen of the UK. This huge palace is over 300 years old and has 775 rooms. Many tourists come to see the Changing of the Guard outside Buckingham Palace. In this famous parade, guards in red jackets march while a band plays music. In August and September each year, Buckingham Palace is open to the public. Then tourists can go inside the Palace and see some of its beautiful rooms and art. This is a chance for people to see inside one of London's most important buildings.

那是威斯敏斯特宫，它是泰晤士河岸边另一座著名的建筑。这座宏伟的建筑有一座高塔，顶部有一个大钟，叫作大本钟。每个整点大本钟都会奏乐报时。四只小一些的钟则每15分钟报一次时。

白金汉宫是英国女王的居所。这座巨大的宫殿有超过300年的历史，拥有775间房间。许多游客来看白金汉宫外的卫兵换岗。在这个著名的仪式里，身着红色制服的卫兵在军乐队的伴奏下完成换班。每年八月和九月，白金汉宫都会向公众开放。这时，游客可以进入这座宫殿，参观其中一些精美的房间，观赏艺术品。对普通民众来说，能进入伦敦最重要的建筑之一参观，实在是一次难得的机会。

37

1. Where is the famous Big Ben? Circle it.

2. Are the following statements True (T) or False (F)?

_____ 1) Tower Bridge can open up when ships pass.

_____ 2) The Tower of London used to be a palace.

_____ 3) The small bells in Big Ben ring every 15 minutes.

_____ 4) Buckingham Palace is open to the public all year round.

Topic Vocabulary 主题词汇

the United Kingdom 英国

the Thames 泰晤士河

Tower Bridge 塔桥

the Tower of London 伦敦塔

the Palace of Westminster 威斯敏斯特宫

Big Ben 大本钟

Buckingham Palace 白金汉宫

the Changing of the Guard 卫兵换岗

Useful Expressions 语汇积累

run through 贯穿

open up 打开

tell the time 报时

open to the public 向公众开放

The bridge goes between two towers. 桥的主体坐落在两座塔楼中间。

This grand building has a tall tower with a clock at the top. 这座宏伟的建筑有一座高塔，顶部有一个大钟。

In this famous parade, guards in red jackets march while a band plays music. 在这个著名的仪式里，身着红色制服的卫兵在军乐队的伴奏下完成换班。

Culture Discovery 文化发现

伦敦气质

伦敦是英国的政治、经济、文化中心，也是一座历史悠久，充满魅力的国际化都市。伦敦和纽约一样也是移民城市，具备了包容、大气、多元的气质。对伦敦的认识应该从人来人往的国王十字火车站开始。众所周知，它是伦敦的铁路交通枢纽之一，主营来往英格兰北部和苏格兰的列车。但很多游客驻足国王十字火车站还有另外一个特殊原因——《哈利·波特》中霍格沃茨特快列车的始发站九又四分之三站台就位于此处。只要你环顾四周，看到有人在排队拍照，那就没错了，排队的人脸上都会洋溢着兴奋而又满足的笑容。

到伦敦不去大英博物馆，那就跟去了北京却没参观故宫博物院一样。世界上有四大著名博物馆，分别是俄罗斯的艾尔米塔什博物馆、纽约大都会博物馆、法国卢浮宫，还有就是伦敦的大英博物馆。它共有近八百万件藏品，精品众多，常年对外展出的就有 5 万多件。大英帝国最鼎盛时期在世界各地搜集的宝藏全都在此，埃及的木乃伊和中国的瓷器都是参观者的最爱。

大英博物馆

国王十字火车站

　　伦敦的贝克街因英国小说家柯南·道尔而闻名。他所塑造的经典侦探人物夏洛克·福尔摩斯就住在贝克街221b号。如今全世界各地的福尔摩斯迷都会去贝克街的福尔摩斯博物馆参观留念，买一些自己喜欢的纪念品，比如福尔摩斯帽、烟斗等。而真正的贝克街221b号现在已收归国有，但每年仍有成千上万的福尔摩斯迷给这个地址写信。

　　坐落于肯辛顿宫边上的海德公园是英国最大最著名的皇家公园，占地2.5平方公里，公园里主要的名胜包括演说者之角、骑马道和戴安娜王妃纪念喷泉。阳光灿烂的时候，海德公园是伦敦市民最喜爱的休闲场所，可以野餐、晒太阳或者慢跑。想要在演说者之角遇到激情四溢的演讲者得需要运气，但是你一定会被英国人悠闲的生活状态所感染，兴许还能遇到一两个在公园里遛狗或骑马的王室成员呢，你要不要去试试？

Think and Answer 问题思考

1. 同样是国际大都市，伦敦和纽约有什么异同呢？
2. 你知道大英博物馆的镇馆之宝有哪些吗？请举例说说。

贝克街 211b 号

海德公园

41

Chapter 2

Tourist Attractions

观光胜地

Unit 5
The Great Wall
长城

The Great Wall

The Great Wall is in the north of China and runs from east to west. In fact, it is not easy to say exactly how long the Great Wall is, because many dynasties built different parts of the wall. The different parts of the wall run in different directions. Also, some parts of the wall are in good condition, and some are not. The total length of the Great Wall is over 20,000 kilometers.

In the past, there were many different states in China. Many states built walls along their boundaries. These walls were made of earth, wood, and stones. During the Qin Dynasty, Emperor Qin Shi Huang joined all the walls together. He did this to stop people from the north invading. This was the beginning of the Great Wall.

长 城

　　长城位于中国北方，横贯东西。实际上，很难确切地说长城究竟有多长，因为许多朝代修建了长城的不同部分。这些部分向不同方向延伸。而且，有些部分保存得很好，有些则没那么幸运。长城的总长超过 2 万公里。

　　古代中国由许多小国组成，这些小国都会沿着国界修筑城墙。这些城墙由泥土、木材和石头建造而成。在秦朝，秦始皇将所有的城墙都连接在一起。他这样做是为了阻止来自北方的侵略者。这就是长城的雏形。

During the Han Dynasty, enemies in the north became stronger. The Han state made the Great Wall longer and stronger.

In the Ming Dynasty, people used stronger building materials, such as bricks, and they built watchtowers along the wall. We can see these parts of the wall today.

The Great Wall is one of the New Seven Wonders of the World. It is also a UNESCO World Heritage Site. Hundreds of thousands of Chinese people built the wall. The wall is a symbol of the strength of the Chinese people. Many parts of the Great Wall still stand today and thousands of people visit it every year.

到了汉朝，北方的敌人更加强大。汉朝便将长城修建得更长、更坚固。

在明朝，人们采用更加坚固的建筑材料，如砖块，并在长城上建造了烽火台。至今我们依然能看到这些烽火台。

长城是世界新七大奇迹之一。它也被联合国教科文组织列为世界遗产地。成千上万的中国人参与修建长城。长城成为中国人民力量的象征。长城的许多段城墙现今仍保存完好，每年吸引着千千万万的游客前往参观。

49

 小小测试

1. Put the following statements in the correct order. Write a-c.

_____ During the Warring States period, many states built walls along their boundaries.

_____ During the Qin Dynasty, Emperor Qin Shi Huang joined all the walls together.

_____ During the Ming Dynasty, people built watchtowers along the wall.

(   ) 2. The Great Wall is in the _____ of China.

   A. south   B. north

(   ) 3. Emperor Qin Shi Huang joined all the walls together to _____.

   A. stop the enemies invading

   B. make friends with other states

(   ) 4. Can you guess why people built watch towers along the wall?

   A. It made the Great Wall more beautiful.

   B. People could send information by it.

Topic Vocabulary 主题词汇

the Qin Dynasty 秦朝

Emperor Qin Shi Huang 秦始皇

the total length 总长

boundary 边界

the Han Dynasty 汉朝

building materials 建筑材料

watchtower 烽火台; 瞭望塔

the New Seven Wonders of the World 世界新七大奇迹

Useful Expressions 语汇积累

run from east to west 横贯东西

run in different directions 向不同方向延伸

in good condition 保存得很好

be made of 由……建造而成

join ... together 将……连接在一起

a symbol of ... ……的象征

In fact, it is not easy to say exactly how long the Great Wall is. 实际上，很难确切地说长城究竟有多长。

He did this to stop people from the north invading. 他这样做是为了阻止来自北方的侵略者。

Many parts of the Great Wall still stand today. 长城的许多段城墙现今仍保存完好。

Culture Discovery　文化发现

秦始皇兵马俑博物馆

很多人去陕西西安的主要目的之一就是参观秦始皇兵马俑博物馆。在中国老百姓心里，它绝对应该被列为世界奇迹之一，而事实上，它也经常被说成是"世界第八大奇迹"。毫不夸张地说，它已成为中国古代文明的一张名片。

秦始皇兵马俑坑坐落于西安临潼区，也位列世界遗产名录。在上世纪 70 年代，一些村民挖井时偶然发现了规模宏大的兵马俑坑，随后的几年里被挖掘出来的物件数量惊人，光大小陶俑就多达 7000 多件，战车 100 多辆，战马 100 多匹。在古代，君王去世后需要陪葬，所谓兵马俑，就是制作成兵马形状样式的殉葬品。秦始皇兵马俑坑较为完好地保留了陵墓的结构体系，对于理解先秦传统和文化有很大的帮助。

三个兵马俑坑以不同军事内容编列，模拟军事作战场景。比如一号俑坑在南边，东西长 216 米，宽 62 米，面积 13260 平方米，以战车和步兵为主；二号俑坑面积 6000 多平方米，以战车、骑兵、弩兵为主。

兵马俑坑

秦始皇兵马俑博物馆

　　亲临兵马俑坑，你一定会被其规模和塑造艺术所震撼，被那些物件和栩栩如生的人物形象所吸引。世人都对秦始皇陵充满了幻想，好莱坞大片里也多次模仿其地宫分布。那么，所谓的秦始皇兵马俑博物馆是否就是秦始皇陵所在地呢？很多人都会将两者混淆，其实博物馆并非秦始皇陵所在地。皇陵也位于临潼区，但在城东 5000 米左右的骊山北麓，这里风景宜人，三面环水，据说非常符合当时建造陵园的要求。目前，中国并未对皇陵进行挖掘，地宫离地很深，工程难度巨大，且会耗费大量的人力物力以及时间，而"世界第八大奇迹"的秦始皇兵马俑博物馆竟然只是皇陵周围挖掘出的陪葬坑之一！

Think and Answer 问题思考

1. 如果有机会去看秦始皇兵马俑博物馆，你最感兴趣的是哪个部分？
2. 除了长城和兵马俑外，你还游览过哪些中国的古迹？贴张照片，写一写。

兵马俑

秦始皇陵

53

Unit 6
West Lake
西湖

West Lake

West Lake, in Hangzhou, is a popular tourist attraction because it is so beautiful. Over hundreds of years, people improved the beauty of this large lake. They created islands and causeways. They created gardens and built pagodas. Visitors can spend hours walking or cycling around West Lake. They can also go for a boat ride.

There are "Ten Views" of West Lake. One of the ten views is "Dawn on the Su Causeway". Early in the morning, visitors can walk along this causeway, through a long line of trees. Another is "Viewing Fish at the Flower Pond". Visitors watch pretty fish come for food. "The Glow of Sunset at Leifeng Pagoda" is the view of this graceful pagoda as the sun goes down.

西湖

　　西湖位于杭州，因其美丽的景致而成为热门的旅游胜地。数百年来，人们不断改造这个大湖，使它变得越来越美丽。人们建造了小岛和堤道、花园和宝塔。游客可以沿着西湖，花上几个小时步行或者骑车游览。他们也可以乘船游览。

　　西湖一共有十景。其中一景便是"苏堤春晓"。一大早，游客们便可以沿着苏堤林荫漫步。另一景是"花港观鱼"。在这里，游客们可以观赏鱼群争食的景象。"雷峰夕照"是指雷峰塔在落日余晖中展现的雄伟景象。

Here is "Snow on the Broken Bridge", another of the Ten Views. During winter, the bridge is covered by snow and it looks broken. When it snows, this bridge and the scenery around it are very beautiful. At the Broken Bridge, people often remember *the Legend of the White Snake*. This is the story of a young man called Xu Xian and two snakes with magical powers—one green, the other white. The two snakes changed into beautiful young women. At the Broken Bridge, it began to rain. Xu Xian lent his umbrella to the young women. Lady White Snake and Xu Xian fell in love and married. Today West Lake is a UNESCO World Heritage Site, both for its beauty and for its cultural history.

West Lake has been a popular place with poets, artists, and storytellers for centuries.

这是十景之一的"断桥残雪"。在冬天，桥被大雪覆盖，看起来像断了一样。下雪时，断桥与周围的景色分外美丽。在断桥上，人们经常会想起《白蛇传》。它讲述了一个名叫许仙的年轻男子和一青一白两条蛇精的故事。这两条蛇精化身成年轻美貌的女子。在雨中的断桥上，许仙将伞借给了这两位年轻女子。后来，白娘子与许仙坠入爱河，并结为夫妻。今天，西湖被联合国教科文组织列为世界遗产地，不仅因为它的美景，也因为它的文化历史。

几个世纪以来，西湖常见于诗人、艺术家与作家的笔下。

Look and match.

● ● The Glow of Sunset at
Leifeng Pagoda

● ● Dawn on the Su Causeway

● ● Viewing Fish at the
Flower Pond

Topic Vocabulary 主题词汇

islands and causeways 小岛和堤道

Ten views of West Lake 西湖十景

Dawn on the Su Causeway 苏堤春晓

Viewing Fish at the Flower Pond 花港观鱼

The Glow of Sunset at Leifeng Pagoda 雷峰夕照

Snow on the Broken Bridge 断桥残雪

the Legend of the White Snake 《白蛇传》

Useful Expressions 语汇积累

tourist attraction 旅游胜地

spend hours doing ... 花上几个小时做……

go for a boat ride 乘船游览

go down 落下

change into ... 化身成……

fall in love 坠入爱河

Visitors can spend hours walking or cycling around West Lake. 游客可以沿着西湖，花上几个小时步行或骑车游览。

Early in the morning, visitors can walk along this causeway, through a long line of trees. 一大早，游客们便可以沿着苏堤林荫漫步。

Visitors watch pretty fish come for food. 游客们可以观赏鱼群争食的景象。

It has been a popular place with poets, artists, and storytellers for centuries. 几个世纪以来，西湖常见于诗人、艺术家与作家的笔下。

Culture Discovery 文化发现

五岳

山水山水，欣赏完著名的"西湖十景"，理应介绍一下山。不论你对名山是不是感兴趣，应该听说过"五岳"吧？五岳皆为道教名山，分别为中岳嵩山、东岳泰山、西岳华山、南岳衡山、北岳恒山。

五岳在历代中国老百姓心里占有不可替代的地位，在漫长的历史过程中，五岳经历了从"高山"到"名山"的演变过程。但凡中国的名山，多少都会受到人文文化的影响，通过与哲学思想、宗教文化等因素结合，最终形成了今日的名胜风景区。

北岳恒山景区内第一胜景当属悬空寺。它建于北魏太和十五年（491年），已经1500多岁了，离地约30层楼高，被誉为建筑美学与宗教的完美融合。悬空寺是纯木打造的，从远处看，整座寺庙仿佛建在几组木头上，其实不然，悬空寺得以吊在空中是因为架在悬崖的栈道上，而栈道下方的悬臂梁才是真正起承重作用的部分。如果你去过悬空寺，一定会感叹它的"奇、玄、险"。此外，悬空寺是"佛、道、儒"三教合一的建筑，

嵩山

恒山

极为罕见，在寺内最高的殿内供奉着佛教创始人释伽年尼、儒家创始人孔子和道家鼻祖老子。

相信你对五岳中的泰山也不会陌生。泰山位于山东省中部，是世界文化与自然双重遗产。五岳被认为是群山之尊，而泰山则是五岳之长，那又是为什么呢？在中国文化里，泰山位于东边，是太阳升起的地方，也是万物起源之地，而泰山神作为泰山的化身，掌管世间万物的出生，被认为是天神和人间沟通的使者。那一句"会当凌绝顶，一览众山小"你一定背诵过吧？杜甫写这首诗的时候才24岁，当时他仕途不顺，考进士没有中，所以开始漫游。途中，他第一次登上了泰山，才有了著名的《望岳》。有机会你一定要登顶泰山，那时可能就能体会那种"世间万物皆过眼云烟"的超然心境了。

Think and Answer 问题思考

1. 你能找到中岳、西岳、南岳的相关文化内容并介绍一下吗？
2. 你还知道哪些关于五岳的诗？能背诵一两首吗？

泰山

华山

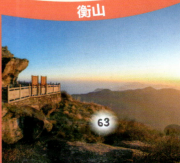

衡山

63

Unit 7
The Pyramids and the Sphinx
金字塔和狮身人面像

The Pyramids and the Sphinx

In the desert near Cairo, in Egypt, there are three huge stone pyramids. They are called the Pyramids of Giza. The ancient Egyptians built them thousands of years ago. The largest pyramid at Giza is called the Great Pyramid. It is 139 meters high. For over 3,800 years, the Great Pyramid was the tallest structure in the world. Why did the ancient Egyptians build these huge pyramids? They were tombs for the pharaohs. The pharaohs were the rulers of ancient Egypt. After a pharaoh died, people made his body into a mummy and put it into a case. People then put the case inside the pyramid.

金字塔和狮身人面像

在埃及开罗附近的沙漠里，有三座巨大的石砌金字塔，它们是吉萨金字塔群。数千年前，古埃及人建造了这些金字塔。吉萨金字塔群中最大的一座叫作大金字塔，它高达139米。在长达3800多年的历史中，大金字塔一直是世界上最高的建筑。古埃及人为什么要建造金字塔呢？金字塔是法老的陵墓，法老是古埃及的统治者。法老死后，人们将他的尸体制作成木乃伊，放入棺材中，随后将棺材放入金字塔中。

The Great Pyramid was the tomb of the pharaoh Khufu. He ruled Egypt around 4,600 years ago. Tens of thousands of people worked for more than ten years to build it. They dragged all of the heavy stones into place.

That large stone statue of an animal is called the Sphinx. It has a lion's body and a human head. The Sphinx sits like a guard in front of the three Pyramids of Giza. In one Greek myth, the Sphinx guarded the city of Thebes. When strangers arrived, the Sphinx asked them a riddle. If people could not give the answer, the Sphinx killed them. The riddle was: "What walks first on four legs, then on two legs, and then on three legs?"

大金字塔是法老胡夫的陵墓。他在大约 4600 年前统治埃及。数以万计的工人用了十多年时间才把大金字塔建造完成。他们将一块块沉重的石头都拖放到预定的位置。

那座巨型动物石像名叫斯芬克斯，也叫"狮身人面像"。它长着狮子的身体，却拥有人的头颅。斯芬克斯正襟危坐，像极了吉萨三座金字塔的护卫。在古希腊的一则神话中，斯芬克斯守卫着底比斯城。有陌生人到访时，斯芬克斯都要让他们猜一个谜语。如果猜不出来，斯芬克斯就会杀了他们。这个谜语就是："什么动物先用四条腿走路，然后用两条腿走路，最后用三条腿走路？"

69

uiz 小小测试

(   ) 1. The pyramids were _____ for the pharaohs.

A. tombs   B. homes

(   ) 2. The largest pyramid at Giza is called _____.

A. the Great Pyramid   B. the Khufu Pyramid

(   ) 3. A mummy is _____ of a pharaoh.

A. the case   B. the body

4. What walks first on four legs, then on two legs, and then on three
legs? _____

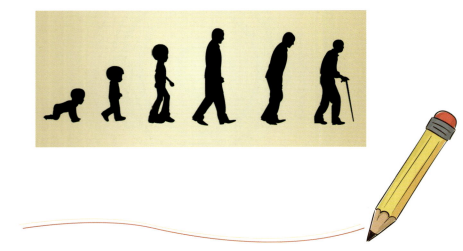

Topic Vocabulary 主题词汇

Cairo 开罗

Egypt 埃及

the Pyramids of Giza 吉萨金字塔群

the Great Pyramid 大金字塔

pharaoh 法老

ruler 统治者

mummy 木乃伊

tomb 坟墓

Sphinx 斯芬克斯（狮身人面像）

Greek myth 希腊神话

the city of Thebes 底比斯城

Useful Expressions 语汇积累

be called ... 被称为 ……

put ... into ... 把 …… 放入 ……

drag ... into ... 把 …… 拖放到 ……

ask somebody a riddle 让某人猜一个谜语

For over 3,800 years, the Great Pyramid was the tallest structure in the world. 在长达 3800 多年的历史中，大金字塔一直是世界上最高的建筑。

The Sphinx sits like a guard in front of the three Pyramids of Giza. 斯芬克斯正襟危坐，像极了吉萨三座金字塔的护卫。

In one Greek myth, the Sphinx guarded the city of Thebes. 在古希腊的一则神话中，斯芬克斯守卫着底比斯城。

Culture Discovery 文化发现

巨石阵

　　埃及的金字塔和狮身人面像充满了异域风情和神秘色彩，但世界上现存的神秘风景名胜还真不仅仅只有金字塔。在爱尔兰、英国、瑞典和北欧一些地方都可以寻觅到巨石阵的踪迹，位于英国威尔特郡索尔兹伯里平原的巨石阵就是其中最著名的遗址之一。

　　索尔兹伯里一马平川的绿色草原上，巍然屹立着一组呈环形的巨石阵，占地约 11 公顷。在巨石阵，周围看不到其他建筑，人们可以全身心投入对遗址的思考。远眺巨石阵，可以欣赏到巨石阵的另外一种美。

　　起初，考古学家估计巨石阵约建于公元前 4000～2000 年，之后陆陆续续的研究发现，巨石阵的建造时间可能在公元前 2300 年左右。没有人能确定当时人们是如何建造巨石阵的，因为它们由巨大的石头组成，每块重达几十吨，还有一些巨石横架在那些巨大的石柱上，所以巨石阵一直在建筑学史上占据着重要的地位。

与此同时，巨石阵在天文学上也有重要的意义。人们发现巨石阵与太阳运行相关，因为它的主轴线、通往石柱的古道和夏至日早晨初升的太阳同在一条线上。另外，其中有两块石头的连线指向冬至日落的方向。所以古人建造巨石阵可能用于观察天象。近年来的研究还发现巨石阵下方有一些纪念碑体，这显然也是人类活动的证明，估计与巨石阵早期的功能有关。

历史学家和考古学家长期以来一直受到一个问题的困扰，那就是巨石阵是不是故意被建成不完整的圆圈呢？至今，这个问题仍然没有确凿的答案。

Think and Answer 问题思考

1. 你认为巨石阵起初就是圆形的吗？为什么？
2. 你知道英国还有哪些著名的古迹吗？

扫码观看完整视频

Unit 8
The Leaning Tower of Pisa
比萨斜塔

The Leaning Tower of Pisa

The Leaning Tower of Pisa is a popular tourist attraction in the Italian city of Pisa. The tower looks like it will fall over, but it has stood for more than 600 years. The tower is actually a bell tower and people started building it in 1173. The tower was straight for the first five years of construction. However, when the builders built the third floor, the tower started to lean. Building stopped for 100 years because there were wars in Italy. They finally finished building the tower in 1372.

In 1989 a bell tower in Pavia, another town in Italy, collapsed. The next year, the Italian government closed the Pisa tower because they were worried about its safety. They spent $30 million to make the tower stable and safe. They did not want to stop it from leaning because it is such a huge tourist attraction. The tower reopened in 2001 and the tourists returned. Today the tower is as popular as ever.

比萨斜塔

比萨斜塔是意大利比萨城一个非常有名的旅游景点。这座塔看起来好像随时都会倒塌，但却屹立了 600 多年。这座塔其实是一座钟楼，始建于 1173 年。在开始建造的前五年里，它还是笔直的。然而，当建到第三层时，整座塔开始倾斜。由于意大利爆发战争，建筑工程停止了 100 年，直到 1372 年才竣工。

1989 年，在意大利一个名叫帕维亚的小镇上，一座钟楼倒塌了。第二年，意大利政府因担心其安全而关闭了比萨斜塔。安全起见，政府耗资三千万美金用来加固比萨斜塔。他们任之倾斜，因为这是一个绝佳的旅游景点。该塔在 2001 年重新开放，吸引了大批游客。如今比萨斜塔一如既往地受人欢迎。

There is a famous story about the tower. A scientist called Galileo dropped two balls from the top of the tower. The balls had the same shape and size, but one was heavier than the other. At that time, scientists believed that a heavier object fell faster than a lighter object. However, when Galileo dropped the two balls, they landed on the ground at the same time. The two balls fell at the same speed. This was an important scientific discovery. Galileo's experiment helped to make the Leaning Tower of Pisa one of the most famous towers in the world.

关于这座斜塔还有一个著名的故事。一个名叫伽利略的科学家从塔顶扔下两个球，两个球有着同样的大小和形状，但一个比另一个要重。当时，科学家都相信较重的物体掉落的速度要比较轻的物体快一些。然而，当伽利略同时扔下这两个球后，它们却同时落地。这两个球下落的速度一样。这是一项非常重大的科学发现。伽利略的实验也使比萨斜塔成为世界上最著名的塔之一。

 小小测试

1. The tower started to lean from the _____ floor.

2. Judge True (T) or False (F).

_____ 1) Building of the tower stopped for 100 years because Italy was out of money.

_____ 2) The tower used to collapse and people rebuilt it.

_____ 3) The government did not stop the tower from leaning because it is a popular tourist attraction.

Topic Vocabulary 主题词汇

the Italian city of Pisa 意大利比萨城

Pavia 帕维亚（意大利小镇）

Galileo 伽利略

scientific discovery 科学发现

bell tower 钟楼

the top of the tower 塔顶

experiment 实验

Useful Expressions 语汇积累

be worried about ... 担心……

stop ... from doing ... 阻止……做……

stable and safe 坚固且安全

at the same time 同时

as popular as ever 一如既往地受人欢迎

The tower looks like it will fall over. 这座塔看起来好像随时都会倒塌。

At that time, scientists believed that a heavier object fell faster than a lighter object. However, when Galileo dropped the two balls, they landed on the ground at the same time. 当时，科学家都相信较重的物体掉落的速度要比较轻的物体快一些。然而，当伽利略同时扔下这两个球后，它们却同时落地。

Galileo's experiment helped to make the Leaning Tower of Pisa one of the most famous towers in the world. 伽利略的实验也使比萨斜塔成为世界上最著名的塔之一。

Culture Discovery 文化发现

古罗马斗兽场

比萨斜塔屹立不倒 600 多年了，已成为意大利的标志性建筑。如果说意大利还有哪些景点能跟比萨斜塔比肩的话，那肯定就是世界闻名的古罗马斗兽场了，它已经俨然成为了一个国家符号和城市象征。

古罗马斗兽场，又被称为"古罗马角斗场"或"古罗马圆形竞技场"，它坐落于意大利首都罗马的市区，是古罗马帝国标志性的建筑。即使你已经知道它有多壮观、磅礴，但真正行走其间，仍会感叹它的雄伟，以及整齐划一的空间排列。同时，你也会敬佩它的巧妙设计。斗兽场占地约 2 万平方米，可同时容纳好几万观众，但因为设计合理，不会出现拥挤不堪的场面，这也就是为什么现在的很多大型竞技场也沿用了其中一些设计的原因。

根据古罗马历史记载，在斗兽场竣工后，当时的上层阶级举办了冷酷而又惨烈的斗兽竞技，既有奴隶与罪犯之间的斗殴，又有猛兽和奴隶之间的决斗。斗兽是当时最为流行的娱乐

活动，上层阶级一般坐在斗兽场的最高一层，既享有最好的视野，又处于安全保护之下。

幸运的是，如今的斗兽场已经不再用于斗兽了，它曾经的历史使命已经完结。现在，它作为一件美丽的建筑艺术品，安静地躺在罗马市区。

另外，在意大利的其他地方也有斗兽场，比如深受海明威喜欢的悬崖之城龙达也有斗兽场。

值得一提的是，意大利建筑风格多样，曾经在欧洲艺术和建筑史上占有重要地位，是建筑爱好者们名副其实的天堂。

Think and Answer 问题思考

1. 意大利古迹众多，除了比萨斜塔和古罗马斗兽场，你还能举出二三个吗？
2. 你知道为什么当时的罗马上层阶级会喜欢斗兽这样的竞技项目呢？